THE EGTA SERIES

New directions in educational guitar music developed by
the UK branch of the European Guitar Teachers Association

General Editor: Richard Wright

Solo Now!
Preparatory Book

**Original Progressive Guitar Solos
in 4 Volumes**

ECH 2100

Visit us on the web at www.chanterelle.com
E-Mail us at chanterelle@chanterelle.com

FOREWORD

For more than a century the guitar has relied on approaches to studies and general learning which, based as they are almost exclusively on solo playing, often leave students with gaps in their technical and musical understanding. Such inflexible conventions are gradually being replaced by much more creative and progressive attitudes among amateur and professional players alike.

The *EGTA Series* with its parallel use of solo and accompanied pieces consolidates and develops these changes methodically and imaginatively, and represents a major contribution to the changing needs of guitar teaching.

John Williams

PREFACE

The aim of this addition to the *Solo Now!* collection is to provide easier and more accessible pieces than those in the previous three volumes. These new solos further minimise the demands made on the left hand so that the student can concentrate on the formation of a stable yet relaxed right-hand position – so vital for the development of a strong and responsive *tirando* technique. All the pieces were designed to be played in the first position so left-hand fingering has been dispensed with altogether. The use of the 4th finger at the 3rd fret, especially on the upper strings, will greatly assist left-hand alignment and is strongly recommended.

Other techniques are also featured here. The *apoyando* stroke can be employed to good effect in bars 18-19 of *Galoshing About* and bars 17-24 of *Little Sad Valse* as well as in the phrased passages of *Regular Reggae, Gimme Five and Beasties. The Persistent Plea* is intended as an introduction to tremolo while *Rising Damp, Regular Reggae* and *Gimme Five* contain simple chords played with the right-hand fingers. *In a Japanese Garden* includes a chord played *tambora* and *Rumba Flamenca* ends with a *rasgueado* flourish.

Varying indications for *laissez-vibrer* or 'over-ringing' are used in the text. Elsewhere every effort should be made to damp open-string bass notes when the harmony changes. Notes to be played staccato (with thumb or fingers) are always followed by a note on the same string. Early planting of the right-hand finger due to play next will easily produce the desired effect.

I would like to thank all those who have contributed material for this book, especially composers new to the project. For their work in developing the ideas which led to the creation of the EGTA Series I would also like to thank Peter Batchelar, John Compton, Luke Dunlea, Stephen Goss, Stuart McGowan, Janet Robinson and Christopher Susans. Over and above the efforts of any individuals, however, the *EGTA Series* is the result of a meeting of minds only made possible by the existence, collective will and organisational capacity of EGTA (UK).

Richard Wright

CONTENTS

1.	Ginette Eady	*Carousel*	4
2.	Richard Wright	*Pas-de-deux*	4
3.	Colin Downs	*A Little Russian Tale*	5
4.	Stephen Kenyon	*Galoshing About*	5
5.	Colin Downs	*Heidi*	6
6.	Richard Wright	*Bicycle Blues*	6
7.	Colin Downs	*My Dog Has Fleas*	7
8.	Ginette Eady	*The Cowboy Trail*	8
9.	Fiona Harrison	*Dragon Dance*	8
10.	Stephen Kenyon	*Rising Damp*	9
11.	Peter Wrieden	*Stanton Moor*	10
12.	Peter Batchelar	*Stepping Out*	10
13.	Derek Hasted	*Regular Reggae*	11
14.	Richard Wright	*The Persistent Plea*	12
15.	Vincent Lindsey-Clark	*Skate on the Lake*	12
16.	Peter Wrieden	*The Lost Abbey*	13
17.	Peter Batchelar	*In a Japanese Garden*	14
18.	Neil Browning	*The Forbidden City*	14
19.	Gareth Glyn	*Sad Song*	15
20.	Peter Wrieden	*Monday Morning Blues*	16
21.	Colin Tommis	*Learning to Tie Shoelaces*	16
22.	Derek Hasted	*Love Song*	17
23.	Peter Wrieden	*The Blacksmith's Boy*	18
24.	Neil Browning	*Play it Cool*	18
25.	Colin Tommis	*Square Pegs, Round Holes*	19
26.	Vojislav Ivanovic	*Little Sad Valse*	20
27.	Richard Corr	*High Life*	21
28.	Gareth Glyn	*Gimme Five*	22
29.	Colin Tommis	*Beasties*	23
30.	Richard Corr	*Rumba Flamenca*	24

Catalogue Number ECH 2100
ISMN M-2047-2100-9
ISBN 978-3-89044-207-5

distributed by:
Chanterelle Verlag, PO Box 103909
D-69029 Heidelberg, Germany

First Published 2008

© 2008 by Michael Macmeeken, Chanterelle Verlag (GEMA) - All Rights Reserved - Manufactured in the EU
This book contains new and original material and is strictly copyright.
No part of it may be reproduced or transmitted in any form or by any means, whether electronic or mechanical,
including photocopying, recording, or by any information storage or retrievel system,
without the prior written permission of the publisher.

Chanterelle® is the registered trade mark of the Chanterelle Verlag, Heidelberg

Music engraved by Richard Wright
Cover design by Ekxakt.de

1. Carousel

Ginette Eady

2. Pas-de-deux

Richard Wright

© 2008 by Michael Macmeeken, Chanterelle Verlag (GEMA)
All Rights Reserved - Manufactured in the EU

3. A Little Russian Tale

Colin Downs

4. Galoshing About

Stephen Kenyon

7. My Dog Has Fleas

Colin Downs

8. The Cowboy Trail

Ginette Eady

9. Dragon Dance

Fiona Harrison

10. Rising Damp

Stephen Kenyon

11. Stanton Moor

Peter Wrieden

Andante (♩ = c.92)

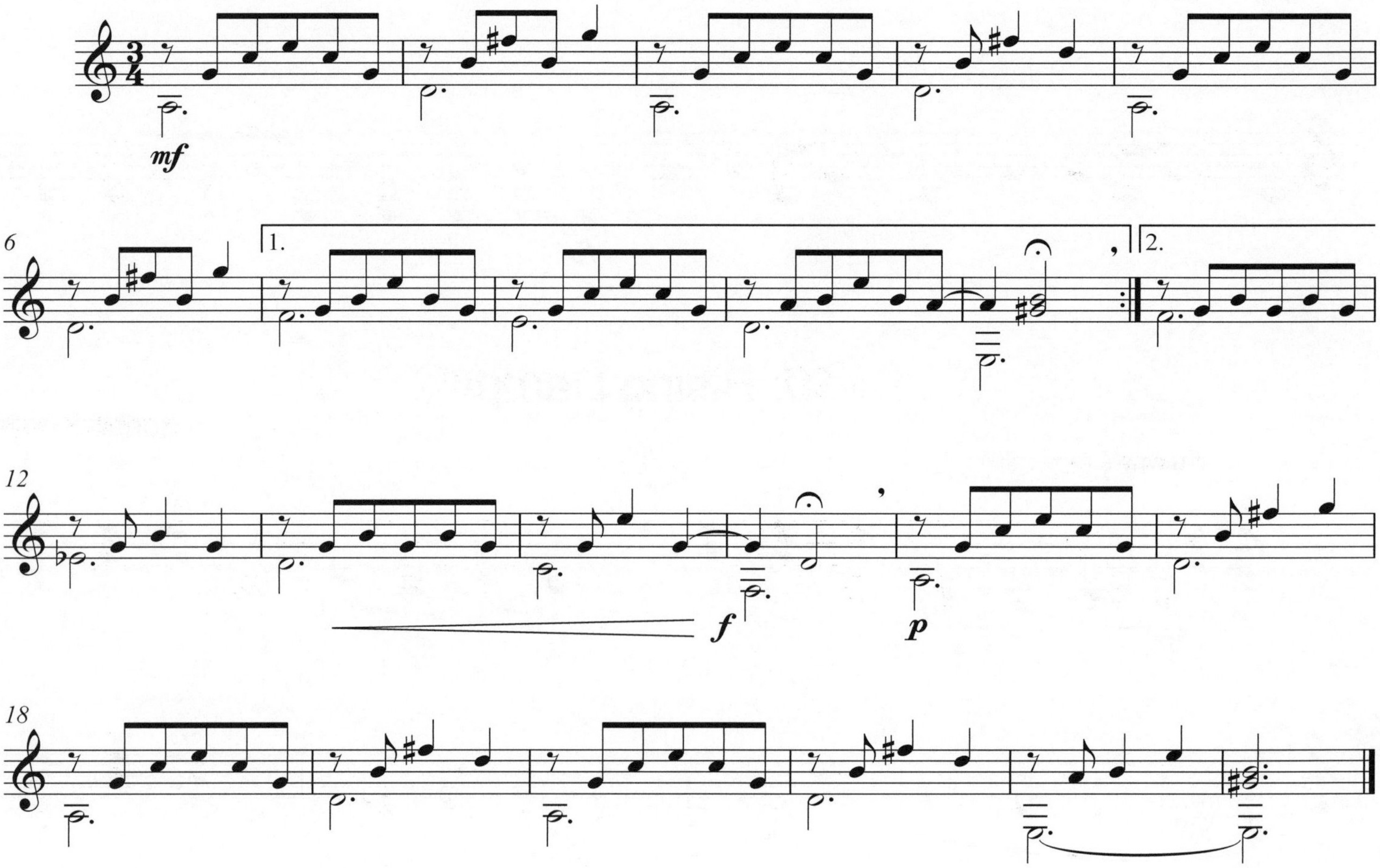

12. Stepping Out

Peter Batchelar

Lively (♩ = c.138)

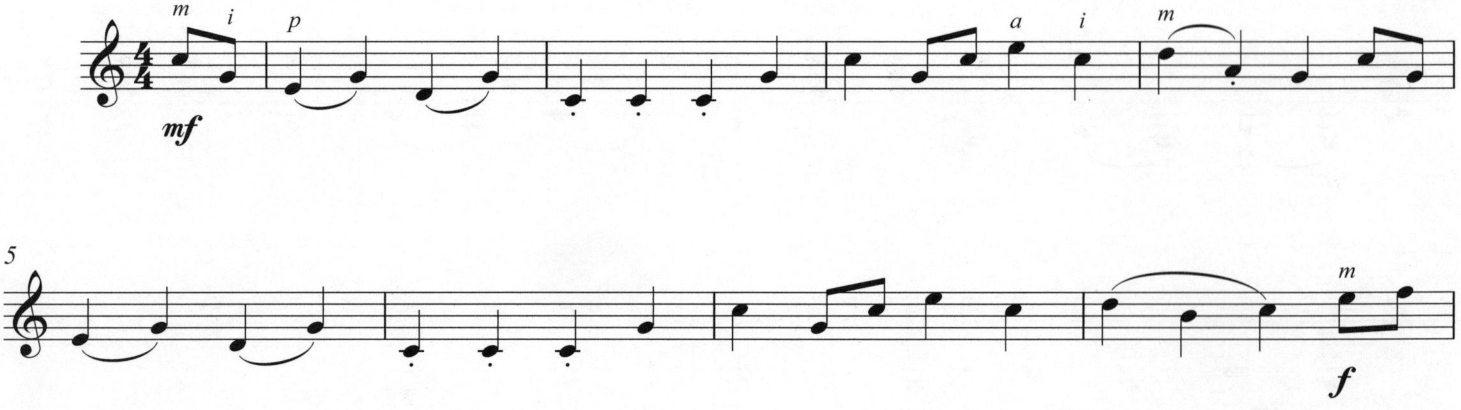

13. Regular Reggae

Derek Hasted

14. The Persistent Plea

Richard Wright

15. Skate on the Lake

Vincent Lindsey-Clark

16. The Lost Abbey

Peter Wrieden

17. In a Japanese Garden

Peter Batchelar

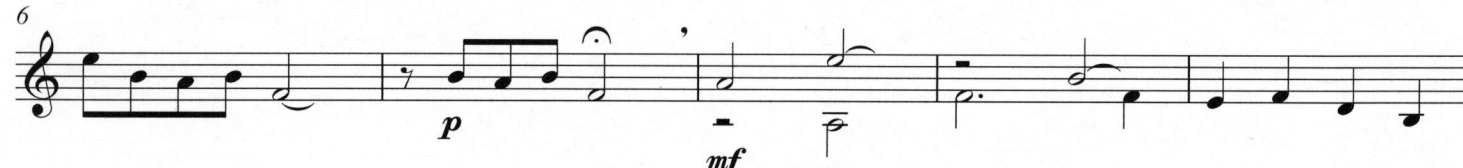

18. The Forbidden City

When China became a republic, the last Emperor, Pu Yi, still a boy, was allowed to live on in his huge palace known as the Forbidden City. A tutor was found for him, a Scotsman called Reginald Johnston. Scottish and Chinese music both use the pentatonic scale; in this piece there are references to 'The Weary Maid', a traditional Scottish tune.

Neil Browning

19. Sad Song

Gareth Glyn

20. Monday Morning Blues

Peter Wrieden

21. Learning to Tie Shoelaces

Colin Tommis

22. Love Song

Derek Hasted

23. The Blacksmith's Boy

A musical dialogue between the blacksmith (a traditional folksong played here in the bass) and his young apprentice.

Peter Wrieden

Broadly (♩ = c.88)

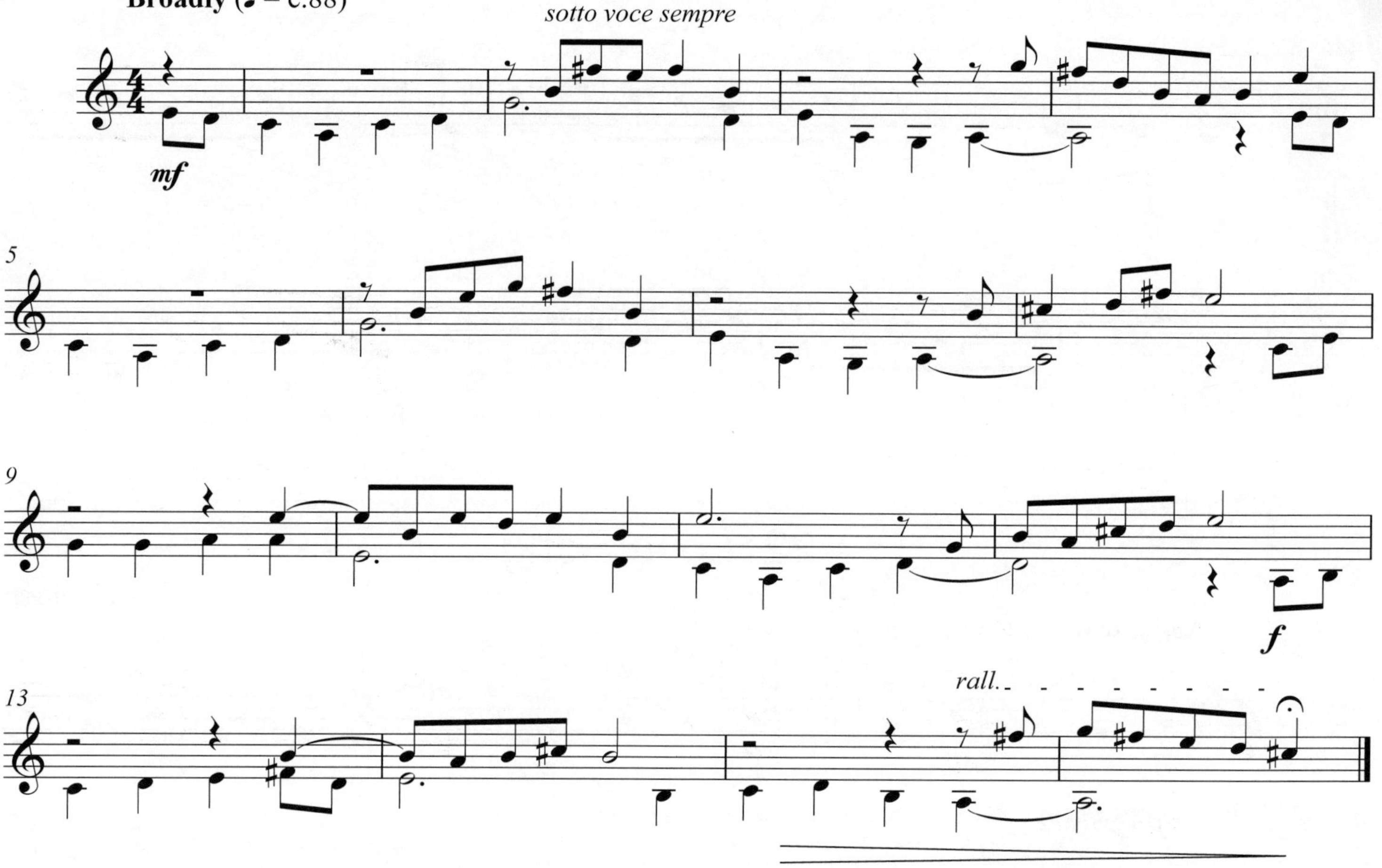

24. Play it Cool

Neil Browning

Steady, with swung quavers (♩ = c.100)

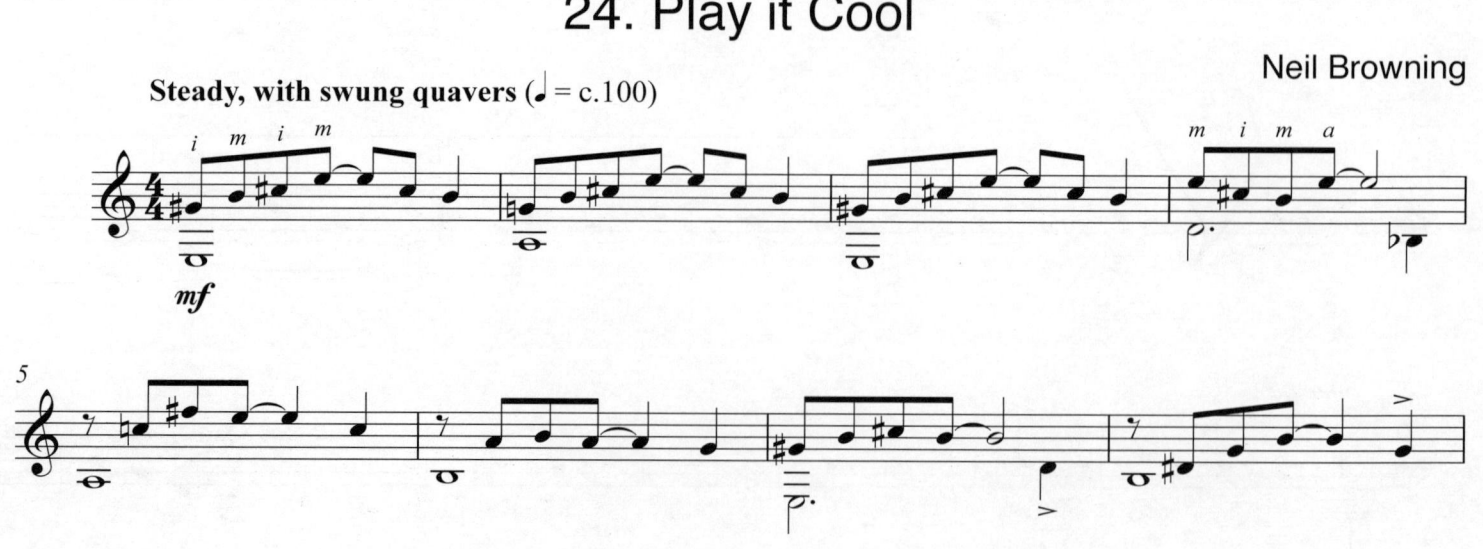

25. Square Pegs, Round Holes

Colin Tommis

Lively (♩ = c.132)

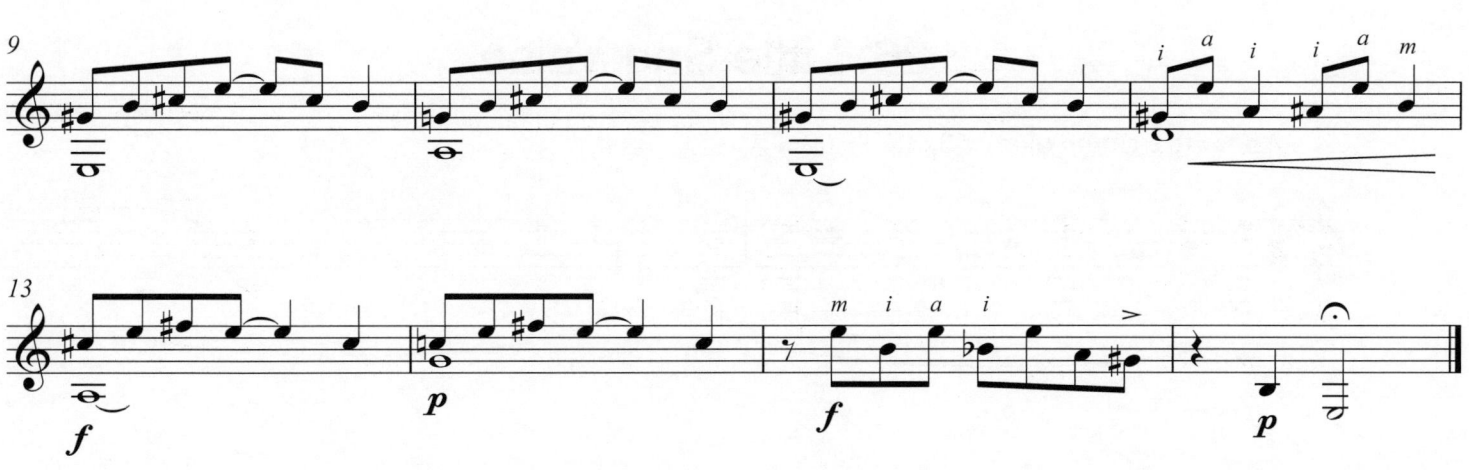

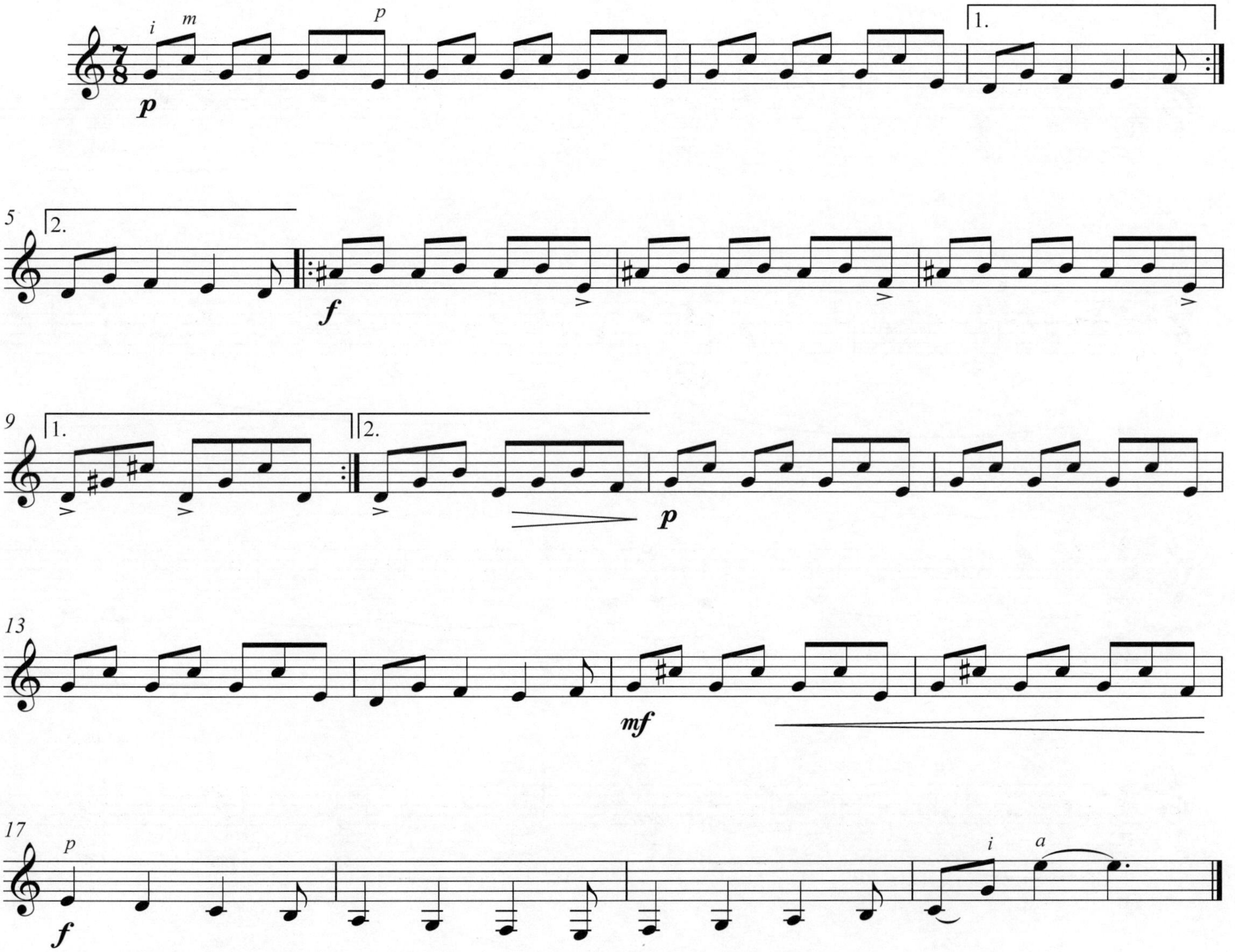

26. Little Sad Valse

Vojislav Ivanovic

27. High Life

Highlife: a type of guitar-based dance music from West Africa.

Richard Corr

28. Gimme Five

Gareth Glyn

29. Beasties

Colin Tommis

30. Rumba Flamenca

Richard Corr